A GUIDE FOR L

The
YOUTHFUL
SEX
OFFENDER

The Rationale and Goals of Early Intervention and Treatment

FAY HONEY KNOPP

SaferSocietyPress

PO BOX 340
BRANDON, VERMONT 05733

Design: Barbara Poeter, Pittsford, Vermont

Typesetting: Amy Rothstein, Waltham, Massachusetts

Readers: Jean Rosenberg, William Stevenson,
          Margaret Stinson, and Lila Tractenberg

Copies of this book may be ordered from:

THE SAFER SOCIETY PRESS
P.O. Box 340
Brandon, VT 05733-0340
(802) 247-3132

$7.00 per copy

ISBN: 1-884444-27-X

CONTENTS

3

FOREWORD

Prior to becoming a juvenile court judge, I handled many adult sex offenders and learned early on that sex offenders do not start at age 18. I learned that their prior sex offenses started when they were adolescents or preadolescents. If we can get to them earlier we are going to prevent a lot of heartache.

In sentencing juvenile sex offenders, the primary issue is community safety. The secondary issue is to decide treatment and punishment issues. Pure punishment without treatment is a real mistake. In prison, sex offenders are the lowest of the social scale. If treatment happens to be available, it is usually optional. Since there is a great deal of victimization of prisoners by other prisoners, I can see sex offenders coming back to society a lot harder and a lot more bitter.

We have also learned that most of the offenders were themselves victims of sexual abuse and that their patterns are similar to those of alcoholics. Unless there is some treatment, they are going to go back to the behavior as they would with any addiction, and they are likely to recidivate. Thus, the earlier the treatment, the better.

Treatment starts with assessment. We insist that there be an assessment by qualified experts, trained psychologists who work for the court. While many psychologists and psychiatrists might be excellent in the fields of mental retardation, paranoia, or schizophrenia, they may have limited knowledge in dealing with sex offenders. The traditional mental health provider may see two or three sex offenders a year and probably is not up to date on the literature, interviewing techniques, evaluation and treatment methods. Therefore, when a defense lawyer presents a report from a psychologist saying there is nothing wrong with his juvenile client, that the sexual offense was a one-time occurrence that has been treated, and that there will be no further behavioral problems, we do not accept it. We insist that our own experienced psychologists do the assessments.

In our Hennepin County Court, in addition to the psychological evaluation, we expect the probation department or the investigating unit of the court to provide a detailed social history. We expect them to meet with the family and the child in the home. We expect that police and child protection reports of the offense will be reviewed and that local police departments will be queried regarding any unreported or unsubstantiated cases that can give us information about the young person. We expect that schools will be perceived as an excellent resource for information. The probation officer is also asked to contact the victim both for input and any information that may have been missed in the police report. These are excellent resources; they provide as much information as possible about that person and we can then make a good disposition.

Though we are not a model for the rest of the country, since every area adapts to its own resources, we are fortunate to live in a large community that has excellent community-based resources and some fine residential treatment programs. Thus, our court is provided with excellent sentencing options.

Basically, cost is not a paramount issue with us. If a child needs treatment, we will find the means to pay for it either through insurance or the county itself picking up the cost. In the court's opinion, as a result of treatment, these young people make some major growth in both sexual awareness and education, and their family relationships are invariably a lot healthier. Their schooling seems to improve, and many are ready to begin again as mature young adults.

ALLEN OLEISKY, *Presiding Judge*
Juvenile Division, District Court
State of Minnesota
May 1, 1985

The Youthful Sex Offender

INTRODUCTION

While it is not possible to estimate accurately the incidence of sexually assaultive behaviors by male youth* in our society, it is clear that such acts are pervasive, drastically underreported, and a cause for our concern (Knopp, 1982). The special problems of juvenile/adolescent sexually abusive male youth have been consistently unacknowledged, neglected, or responded to inappropriately. Often, such behaviors are dismissed as sexual curiosity or experimentation, interpreted as purely situational in nature, or excused because they are perceived as normal aggressiveness of a sexually maturing adolescent. Unfortunately, as a result, no intervention occurs at the most crucial stage in the early development of the sex offender—when he first begins to exhibit the symptoms of pathology and before his assaults have become ingrained and less responsive to treatment (Groth & Loredo, 1981).

Thus, one completely inappropriate response to a youth who has demonstrated sexually aggressive behavior is to do nothing about it, to ignore it, not to demand accountability and responsibility from him for his actions. An equally inadequate response is to incarcerate the youngster with no provisions for treatment, expecting that some-how punishment will teach him a lesson and the behavior might stop. Other common, but unsatisfactory, responses include sentencing the youngster without benefit of a competent clinical assessment by an experienced sex-offender evaluator, or sentencing the offender to tra-ditional *non*specialized therapy in whatever type of program happens to be available, regardless of his placement needs.

---

* This publication does not address the phenomenon of assaultive sex offenses by adolescent females.

In contrast, the optimum judicial response to the youthful sex offender's behavior is:

1) To pay attention to the behavior and demand accountability from the young person;

2) To provide specialized sex-offender assessment, evaluation, and treatment in order to interrupt the behavior therapeutically as early as possible;

3) To select the proper placement from a range of treatment settings, including community-based non-residential through secure residential, followed by post-treatment services.

While the incidence of adolescent sex offenses continues to be significantly underreported in official statistics, there is increasing awareness of the extent of the problem and the need for early specialized therapeutic intervention. This is especially noted in the recent marked growth in the number of treatment services available to these clients nationwide.

Though 47 states offer some type of private or public treatment for these young clients,[1] very few states provide comprehensive assessment, treatment, and post-treatment services. As a result, courts usually have limited treatment options available; and thus young sex offenders may be placed in settings highly inappropriate to their treatment and custodial needs.

From a community safety perspective, it is crucial that persons in the judicial, legislative, and other public and private agencies understand the need for early therapeutic intervention in sexually assaultive behaviors. *The Youthful Sex Offender* addresses some of the complex issues involved in such intervention. The next five sections 1) summarize the rationale for early remedial intervention in adolescent sex offenses, 2) provide some guidelines for determining

---

[1] The Safer Society Program maintains state listings of identified adolescent and adult treatment providers and programs.

whether the behavior was "normal" or inappropriate, 3) identify some clinical risk criteria, 4) review six program goals for assessing and treating young sex offenders, and 5) suggest ten recommendations to assist states in planning a comprehensive response to the problem of adolescent sex offenses.

Section One

RATIONALE FOR EARLY INTERVENTION

SEXUAL ASSAULTS BY ADOLESCENTS ARE grossly underreported by both the victims of such assaults and in official statistics (Knopp, 1982). Data from other than official sources, however, reflect the seriousness of the problem. Programs serving child and adult victims of sexual abuse, for instance, provide some striking statistics on the sexual victimization of boys and girls by adolescents. Some centers report up to 56 percent of the assailants as under age 18 (Knopp, 1982).

Treatment programs for youthful and adult sex offenders also have produced important data. Extraordinary numbers and diversity of hitherto unreported sexually aggressive acts have been discovered in the life histories of such clients along with evidence of 1) the early onset of the behaviors, and 2) the potential for escalation in the seriousness of the offenses among many adolescents.

INCARCERATED OFFENDER DATA

In one study of incarcerated adult rapists and child molesters (Groth, Longo, & McFadin, 1982), for example, the offenders admitted to committing up to five times as many sexual offenses as those for which they were apprehended. Child molesters committed their first offense as early as eight years of age and rapists as early as nine years of age.

A study with a similar population (Longo & Groth, 1982) reflects the potential for escalation from hands-off to hands-on sexually aggressive behaviors when no treatment intervention is made. Of the incarcerated adult sex offenders interviewed, 35 percent reported progression from compulsive masturbatory activity, repetitive exhibitionism, and/or persistent voyeurism as juveniles, to the more serious behaviors for which they were convicted as adults.

Data drawn from the adolescent sex-offender population at Hennepin County Home School in Minnesota, a residential treatment program described in *Remedial Intervention in Adolescent Sex Offenses* (Knopp, 1982), reveal a similar high incidence and variety of sexually aggressive behaviors among some clients. In self-reports collected from clients anonymously, for example, one adolescent admitted to 30 rapes and 30 "indecent liberties" with victims at least three or more years younger, voyeurism, and incest involvements with a brother, nephew, and niece (Haversack, 1984).

NONINCARCERATED OFFENDER DATA

While incarcerated populations may consist of more serious compulsive clients, data from nonincarcerated, sex-offender populations reveal similar findings.

In a unique study drawn from 411 nonincarcerated sex offenders who volunteered for outpatient treatment under guaranteed conditions of strict confidentiality (Abel, Mittelman, & Becker, 1983), about half of the clients experienced deviant arousal as adolescents and many developed their interest when they were 12 years old or younger.

These data confirmed also that many sex offenders do not confine themselves to a single type of deviant behavior and that the behaviors may increase in number and often escalate in seriousness as the offender grows older. Approximately 50 percent of the men had multiple deviations. Of a sample of 89 rapists, for instance, half were involved also in pedophilia, almost 30 percent were involved in exhibitionism, 20 percent were involved in voyeurism, and 12 percent in frottage.

Startling data on the number and types of victims involved in assaults by sex offenders emerged in this study. The 232 child molesters were responsible for a total of 17,585 victims, many of whom were young males. These child molesters produced more than 10 times the number of victims than the rapists. The young male victims were more than 11 times as likely to be molested outside the family than the young female victims. Since sexually abused young men can be considered a high-risk population (because each carries a strong potential for becoming a sexual victimizer himself), the capability for swift victim intervention to help break this possible cycle of sexual aggression should be an important prevention and public policy concern.

Never before has there been such stunning empirical evidence to demonstrate the need for early therapeutic intervention in the sexually aggressive behaviors of young males. According to Gene Abel and his colleagues, the average adolescent male sex offender in their study could affect 380 victims during his lifetime, reflecting an increase of 55 times in the number of victims as the offender moves from adolescence to adulthood. Abel warns: "If you do not get them in treatment—this is what will happen."

THE PRICE OF NONINTERVENTION

An examination of some of the patterns of adult sex offenders demonstrates "what can happen" if specialized therapeutic intervention is not available to young offenders. From an early age (generally 11 or 12 years old), many sex offenders develop specific interest in various sexual behaviors. It cannot be stated with scientific certainty *why* such patterns develop, but many agree that aggressive sexual behaviors are learned primarily through observation and by direct experience. Cultural influences, the socialization process, chaotic, enmeshed, or rigid families, imbalances of power and status, or early childhood experiences, particularly those involving sexual trauma, may be important factors in this learning process. Data from adolescent treatment programs, for instance, indicate that the majority of sex offenders (usually from 60 to 100 percent) report experiencing some form of early sexual victimization. Such experiences are thought to contribute to some types of later sexually aggressive behaviors, particularly those involving sexual attraction to children.

Chronic and compulsive sex offenders, or "paraphiliacs,"[2] usually begin their deviant sexual interests at an early age, fantasize, and reinforce the deviant themes during masturbation and orgasm. That, explains Abel (1984), is a critical development and the key to their developing a *persistent* deviant arousal:

> When you see these kids by the time they have committed a few crimes, they have already started to use and associate these deviant fantasies with orgasm. That has to be disrupted early [or it can become] *chronic*. When the problem becomes chronic, it takes on a life in and of itself because now a few activities are used hundreds and perhaps thousands of times as they relive those highly erotic experiences. When there is a pairing or association between those fantasies and orgasm, that welding together, that chronicity, makes the problem much more difficult to deal with. Trying to unglue that by the time they are 30 or 40 years old is a major undertaking. It can be done, but if you had your druthers you wouldn't. It would be better to approach them when they are younger.

Because of the problem of chronicity in sexual offenses, specialists who are veterans of treating adult sex offenders never mention the word "cure"— only "control" or "reduction." These compulsive behaviors are compared often to other addictive, habitual behaviors such as alcohol abuse and patterns associated with obesity, gambling, and drug dependency. "Any behavior that is compulsive, heavily patterned, and ritualized always remains in the behavioral repertoire," says Roger Wolfe of Northwest Treatment Associates in Seattle (Knopp, 1984). "It is always there, it can be relearned, re-energized or reinitiated at any time. You may learn a new behavior that competes

---

[2] Paraphiliacs find unusual or bizarre imagery or acts necessary for sexual excitement, and their behavior tends to be involuntarily repetitive. The paraphilias include pedophilia, exhibitionism, voyeurism, sexual masochism, sexual sadism, fetishism, transvestism, zoophilia, frotteurism, and telephone scatologia. See American Psychiatric Association, 1980, pp. 226-227 and 275.

The Youthful Sex Offender

with or suppresses the deviant one; you may unlearn it, but you will not erase it." Thus, intervention in these patterns *before* they become chronic is extremely important.

Finally, it is obvious that specialized community-based treatment in low-risk cases, provided at the earliest recognition of the problem or at the time of first legal involvement, is much less expensive than later institutional treatment for more serious offenses. In 1991 the annual per-client cost in a specialized sex-offender community-based program was approximately $900 per year. In the same period the annual cost to incarcerate one juvenile in a secure Division for Youth facility was approximately $80,000. Costs would be similar today. Thus, *fiscally* we cannot afford *not* to provide early remedies, nor can we afford it for safety reasons.

Thus, the rationale for early therapeutic intervention in juvenile and adolescent sexually aggressive behavior is clear and compelling: 1) deviant patterns are less deeply ingrained and are therefore easier to disrupt; 2) youth are still experimenting with a variety of patterns of sexual satisfaction which offer alternatives to consistent deviant patterns; 3) distorted thinking patterns are less deeply entrenched and can be redirected; 4) youth are good candidates for learning new and acceptable social skills; 5) public safety is improved by preventing further victimization; and 6) fiscal economy is enhanced.

Section Two
"NORMAL" OR INAPPROPRIATE BEHAVIOR? SOME GUIDELINES

WHEN A YOUTH IS REFERRED to a clinician for evaluation of sexual behavior, one of the clinical tasks is to differentiate among 1) what may be normative sexual activity, 2) what may be inappropriate solitary sexual activity of a nonaggressive nature, and 3) what may be sexually assaultive behavior that poses some risk of harm to another person. The first is a social matter, the second a clinical matter, and the third is a clinical and legal matter (Groth & Loredo, 1981).

A useful document by Groth & Loredo (1981) summarizes eight issues key to the evaluation of a sexually abusive adolescent.

1. What is the age relationship between the persons involved? Are they peers or agemates, or is one of the individuals significantly older or younger than the other? The greater the discrepancy in age, the more inappropriate the sexual activity, especially where the postpubertal youth is involved with a prepubertal child.

2. What is the social relationship between the persons involved? While nonconsensual sexual behavior by the adolescent is always inappropriate, the meaning behind the social relationship, or lack of it, needs to be explored.

3. What type of sexual activity is being exhibited? Are the sexual acts consistent with the developmental level of the youth, or do they appear to reflect more advanced knowledge or experience than would be expected of someone that age? Is the activity unusual or unconventional in any respect, and does it appear to have any symbolic meaning? Are there any ritualistic elements involved in the sexual activity? When the type of sexual activity exhibited by the juvenile is either age-inappropriate, socially inappropriate, or ritualistic, it may signify the use of sex to express nonsexual needs and issues operating in the youth and the undermining of his psychosexual development. In such cases it is crucial to explore carefully the youth's fantasies that accompany such sexual activities.

4. How does the sexual contact take place? Is it through mutual agreement and negotiation, or does one person gain sexual access to the other through deception and enticement, entrapment or intimidation, threat or physical force? The only permissible type of sexual encounter is a consenting one. Any other way of gaining sexual access to a person is inappropriate and cause for concern.

Sexual encounters that are not based on mutuality, reciprocity, and consent constitute assaults. Clinicians should not minimize a juvenile or adolescent sexual offense as simply the reflection of a socially inept and sexually awkward youth, but should recognize it as an offense and carefully examine the interrelationships of sexuality and aggression in the dynamics.

5. How persistent is the sexual activity? Compulsive sexual activity and/or adolescent involvement in a range of inappropriate sexual behaviors suggest that the adolescent may be experiencing some overwhelming stresses and tensions. The clinician should explore how often and the length of time the activity has been occurring; whether it appears to be an excessive preoccupation and persistent activity that predominates in the adolescent's behavior; and whether or not it has a compulsive, driven quality.

6. Is there any evidence of progression in regard to the nature or frequency in the sexual activity? Has the activity changed over time? Is it becoming more frequent or elaborate? Is any type of pattern or ritual emerging? Have any changes been noted in regard to the type of sexual acts performed, the type of person the sexual acts are directed toward, and/or the way in which sexual contact is achieved? Any indications of an increase in aggression over time should be perceived as ominous.

7. What is the nature of the fantasies that precede or accompany the adolescent's abusive behavior? The adolescent's sexual fantasies may offer clues to his own self-image, his comfort or discomfort with his own sexuality, the nature of his sexual interests, and the quality of his interpersonal relationships and other important information.

8. Are there any distinguishing characteristics about the persons who are targets of the adolescent's assaults? In addition to age and social relationships already mentioned, attention should be given to any encounters in which a person is targeted because s/he may be handicapped, disadvantaged, or vulnerable.

Any given sex offense may cut across all types of conventional diagnostic classifications. The offense itself is not a diagnostic category, it is a behavioral act. The evaluation of the sexually abusive adolescent, then, requires not only that the sex offense be assessed carefully, but that this behavior be examined in regard to the offender's personality development and in the context of his current life, particularly his family situation. In addressing these issues, Groth & Loredo suggest three general queries:

1. What critical developmental events or experiences may have combined to predispose the adolescent to act out his problem? It is especially important to determine whether he himself was ever the victim of a sexual assault or other sexual trauma. Does his offense constitute (in part) an unsuccessful and maladaptive effort to work through his sexual trauma? Is he attempting to counter the impact of being a helpless victim by becoming a powerful victimizer? Is he retaliating or "getting even" for being victimized and in this way validating or restoring his sense of manhood?

2. What current life tensions or stresses, particularly family dynamics, are operating on him that serve to trigger the offense? Clinicians need to determine (a) the nature of the interrelationships among the members of the adolescent's family and how the dynamics affect him; (b) the characteristic family attitudes and behaviors that serve to precipitate or perpetuate his sex offenses; (c) his primary role models in regard to sexual and aggressive behaviors; and (d) the prevailing attitude or reaction of his parents toward his sex offense, such as minimization and denial, guilt induction, physical punishment, and whether they fail to address the underlying problems and react only to the symptom.

3. To what extent are the adolescent sex offender's problems compounded by other serious disorders such as retardation, mental illness (psychosis), drug or alcohol dependency, organicity,[3] and so forth? What is the primary problem and what is the secondary behavior?

[3] Organicity is the attribution of diseases, particularly mental disorders, to organic diseases or lesions.

Section Three
CRITERIA FOR ASSESSING RISK

ONCE THE APPROPRIATENESS OF INTERVENTION is determined by qualified clinicians, what type of criteria exist to help determine the risk to community safety if the sexually abusive youth is treated in a non-residential program?

A 62-point checklist of criteria relating to appropriateness of outpatient versus residential treatment was developed by staff of the Juvenile Sexual Offender Program at the University of Washington School of Medicine's Adolescent Clinic.[4] "The Juvenile Sexual Offender Decision Criteria" is not validated by research and therefore should be considered as a guide. Further, the list is helpful only when used by specialized and experienced sex-offender evaluators in conjunction with other clinical data.

Wayne Smith, Director of Research at the program, suggests four distinct clusters of items to be considered when assessing youthful sex offenders for placement: 1) seriousness of referral offense; 2) treatability/manageability of offender; 3) probability of sexually reoffending (with and without recommended intervention); and 4) likely danger to the community, with and without recommended intervention (Smith, 1985).

---

[4] An original 37-point checklist, authored by Gary Wenet and Toni Clark in 1977, is included in *Remedial Intervention in Adolescent Sex Offenses* (Knopp, 1982), pp. 32-33. The Juvenile Sexual Offender Program is no longer functioning.

Some of the common high-risk factors that indicate the inappropriateness of youthful sex offenders for community treatment might include: 1) it was a repeated offense for which the offender had already received treatment; 2) the offense involved violence, physical force, use or threat of use of a weapon; 3) evidence of progressive increase in the force used to commit a repeated offense; 4) the offense was predatory, ritualistic, or continued despite the victim's expression of distress; and 5) the offender's significant intellectual deficits limit his ability to learn from the consequences of his behavior.

Thus, for the courts, there are at least two requisites for safe and sound dispositions of adolescent sex-offender cases. First, that competent and specialized assessment and evaluation are available for these young offenders so that both risk and the nature of treatment can be determined, and second, that a wide range of treatment settings are in place so that appropriate placement can be selected.

Section Four
GOALS & METHODS OF TREATMENT

UNTIL THE FALL OF 1975, when the University of Washington School of Medicine's Adolescent Clinic was asked to evaluate and treat a group of adolescent sex offenders, sex-offense evaluation and treatment had not been undertaken in the United States for this age group in a coherent and comprehensive fashion. While the number of community and residential programs and service providers has grown steadily, of the 660 identified services, seven states claim credit for almost half of them.[5]

Community-based services for sexually abusive youth are inexpensive to implement, since they do not require capital investment for new physical plants. Treatment occurs in such diverse settings as converted houses or schools, hospital outpatient wings, mental health centers, professional offices, and university or religious social service centers.

The length of treatment can range from a low of four weeks for "borderline" incidents which require some educational exposure, to one or more years. Most community-based programs, however, range from six months to one year.

Length of sessions range from a low of one hour (much too short) to three or more hours per week, plus time spent on homework

---

[5] The states are CA, WA, OH, NY, MA, MI, and OR.

and additional sessions where family therapy is involved. Clients range in age from eight to 18 years, but are predominately 14 to 17 years of age.

Residential programs, located in state schools or facilities under the care of various youth agencies, range from "open" to "secure." Usually sex offenders live in the general population and meet in separate offense-specific groups at least one or more times per week. Those programs that maintain separate cottages for sex offenders believe such arrangements provide considerable advantages for both staff and residents and create a needed, intensive-change milieu.

At the present time, what can be referred to as "the new sex-offender assessment and treatment discipline" is being painstakingly hammered out on a day-by-day basis within the confines of adult and adolescent treatment programs and in a few research laboratories.

The teaching of this highly eclectic, rapidly evolving, and multimodal discipline is glaringly absent from the traditional curricula of schools of medicine, nursing, mental health, and social work. Rather, it is being transferred informally through conferences, treatment-related state and county networks, and focused training sessions. Thus, each state needs to develop a capacity to train professionals in this new and important discipline.

The new adolescent sex-offender discipline includes a variety of psychotherapeutic, cognitive, and behavioral elements and incorporates a wide range of educational and training components. A biomedical component, Depo-Provera,[6] which lowers sexual drive, is offered to adolescents in seven percent of the programs specializing in such treatment (Knopp & Stevenson, 1990).

The concept of treatment is an integrated one. Assessment of the adolescent sex offender, for example, is perceived not only as an initial part of treatment but as a continuing strategy. Similarly, on the other end of the spectrum, in residential programs, exiting or post-release strategies are viewed as an extension of the total treatment plan.

---

[6] The hormonal drug Depo-Provera (Medroxyprogesterone Acetate) is used to suppress the production of the male hormone testosterone as a means of curbing sex drive and sexual fantasies. It is used in conjunction with other treatment methods.

The Youthful Sex Offender

Practitioners shape their programs by selecting various combinations of assessment and treatment approaches from this broad repertoire of psychotherapeutic, cognitive, and behavioral components. In the majority of programs, guided peer-group therapy, usually co-led by a woman and a man, forms the core of the program design. Peer-group therapy can be supplemented by individual therapy, and, where parents and siblings are available, a very strong family therapy component is advocated. In some programs, family therapy forms the core of the program design, supplemented by group and individual therapy.

The methods of assessing and treating adolescent sex offenders are variously applied in residential and nonresidential programs, depending on the severity of the behavior. Intensity of programming and structure increases in line with severity of the offense or longevity of the behavior. Six comprehensive treatment goals are identified here, and some of the approaches that are used to fulfill these goals are briefly stated.[7]

GOAL ONE

Each adolescent sex offender needs a complete, individualized assessment and treatment plan. The population that commits sexual offenses is extremely heterogeneous. Since there is no succinct profile to describe the adolescent sex offender, initial and ongoing assessments are prerequisites for determining individual treatment needs.

There are substantial differences between the assessment of youthful sex offenders and clients with more traditional mental health problems. These differences are elaborated upon in *Retraining Adult Sex Offenders: Methods & Models* (Knopp, 1984); however, it is important to note that within the traditional mental health profession there is a tendency toward seriously underestimating the risks involved with sex offenders.

---

[7] For further information see Knopp, 1982, 1984; Knopp & Stevenson, 1989; also see National Adolescent Perpetrator Network, 1988.

In addition to in-depth clinical interviews, assessment approaches include paper and pencil tests for the youth's most common cognitive distortions; psychological and psychosocial testing of personality, intelligence, and ability; psychosexual testing and sexual knowledge inventories; social and empathy skills testing; various instruments to measure family dynamics; and sometimes, physiological monitoring of arousal patterns (strain gauge measurements of penile erection response). Compared to adult treatment programs, fewer evaluators of adolescent sex offenders use physiological measurements. However, those who do contend that assessments are more accurate and economical in terms of time spent and range of paraphilias identified.

Adolescents should be asked always about their involvement in all paraphilias, not only the behavior that has come to the attention of the court. If general questions are asked, the adolescent is very likely to respond with general answers and conceal various paraphilias since the behaviors are illegal and he may feel embarrassed. The adolescent's penile erection response to various stimuli on video or audiotapes, slides, pictures, and card sorts, may disclose discrepancies between self-report test results and initial clinical histories. Judith Becker, Director of the Sexual Behavior Clinic at the New York State Psychiatric Institute, reports that after such discrepancies emerged during assessment, 62.2 percent of those interviewed (80 adults and 10 adolescents) reported additional, paraphiliac arousals (Becker & Abel, 1984).

GOAL TWO

Each sex offender needs to (a) accept responsibility for the offenses in which he has been involved and (b) have an understanding of the sequence of thoughts, feelings, events, circumstances, and arousal stimuli that make up his "offense syndrome" that precedes his involvement in sexually aggressive behaviors. These are called variously "links in the offense chain of events," "offense antecedents," or "offense precursors." Given the tendency of sex offenders to deny, minimize, rationalize, or lie about their sexually assaultive behaviors, getting them to own and accept responsibility for their acts is one of the first elements in the treatment agenda.

Some programs will not accept offenders if, during their interview or orientation period, they refuse to be honest and continue to shift blame elsewhere, or insist that because of drugs or alcohol they cannot remember the incident. Other programs, particularly the residential ones, might work with a young offender for up to a year before getting him to take responsibility for his behavior.

A combination of psycho-socioeducational modules, cognitive, Rational-Emotive, Gestalt, Transactional Analysis, insight-oriented, and behavioral approaches are employed in getting the offender to become familiar with his offense antecedents—the chain of factors that he personally activates prior to his offending. For the majority of offenders, this task is less complicated when the offender is young. At that age he is more closely in touch with his feelings and experiences, and his fantasies are less ingrained.

To help the clients learn their preoffense patterns, programs may use group and individual sessions, the writing of autobiographies and wall charts, journal and log keeping, and physiological assessments of sexual arousal patterns.

If individual preoffense patterns are identified in the offender's file, specially trained probation and parole officers can recognize a particular offender's early warning signals and help him to intervene in any drift toward reoffending.

GOAL THREE

Each sex offender needs to learn how to (a) intervene in or break into his offense pattern at its very first sign and (b) call upon the appropriate methods, tools, or procedures he has learned in order to suppress, control, manage, and stop the behavior. The first step in breaking into the offense pattern is to recognize the earliest link in the chain of thoughts, feelings, and events that lead to offending.

Control techniques range from least intrusive to the most intrusive methods: from relaxation and stress-management techniques, to thought-stopping, thought-shifting, impulse-charting, various cognitive deterrents, and cognitive restructuring; and progress to stronger interventions such as removing oneself from the high-risk situation or having others monitor removal; to various aversion/behavioral suppression methods. These behavioral interventions might include covert sensitization, cognitive aversive conditioning, masturbatory satiation, and olfactory aversion, all methods of suppressing deviant arousal. Most programs use an eclectic approach and provide a broad range of intervention tools to the sex offender who can use them if he chooses to.

GOAL FOUR

Each sex offender needs to engage in a reeducation and resocialization process in order to (a) replace antisocial thoughts and behaviors with prosocial ones, (b) acquire a positive self-concept and new attitudes and expectations for himself, and (c) learn new social and sexual skills to help cultivate positive, satisfying, pleasurable, and nonthreatening relationships with others.

The reeducation and resocialization agendas in adolescent sex-offender treatment programs are implemented through selection from a wide array of methods to meet the offender's individual needs and deficits. These resocialization opportunities may include 1) changing culturally rooted stereotypic notions about the roles of women and men in our society; 2) overcoming myths and misperceptions about human sexuality, and increasing nondeviant, positive sexuality; 3) dealing with the sexual, physical, and emotional victimizations the offender may have suffered personally as a youth; 4) learning empathy, victim awareness, and how to build caring relationships with others; 5) learning assertiveness skills to manage appropriately and to express anger and other negative or positive feelings; 6) improving self-esteem; 7) increasing living, educational, and vocational skills; and 8) learning strategies for controlling alcohol and drug abuse.

As previously noted, there is no succinct "profile" of the adolescent sex offender, and many young people with similar backgrounds do *not* sexually offend against others. Nevertheless, some striking commonalities about sex offenders point to important issues to address in treatment and prevention. Two deserve special mention here.

First, among sex offenders, none has yet been reported to have a warm, close, nurturing, and gentle relationship with his father (Knopp, 1982). Fathers seems to be either abusive or physically or emotionally absent for these young people. Thus, while many programs place a strong emphasis on redefining roles of women, an important emphasis on nurturing relationships with men is also emerging. This focus addresses a need that was never met in the adolescent sex offenders' lives.

A second commonality among adolescent sex offenders that is difficult to overlook is the great confusion about sexuality in general and positive sexuality in particular. The Minnesota adolescent sex-offender treatment programs are admirable in their emphasis on addressing the perception in our culture that sex is degrading and dirty. If sexuality is devalued, then it can be used to degrade or humiliate another person, and sexuality becomes the means of expression of nonsexual needs.

While many programs offer traditional kinds of sex education, only a few programs educate about positive, pleasurable, and appropriate sexuality. If an offender is expected to relinquish behavior which, though inappropriate, provides him with a great deal of pleasure, he needs to be schooled in finding more appropriate and pleasurable sexual behavior.

GOAL FIVE

Each high-risk, residential sex offender needs a prolonged period during his treatment when he can begin to test safely his newly acquired insights and control mechanisms in the commu-

nity, without the potential for affronting or harming members of the wider community.

The period of release into the community is the most challenging and crucial to the sex offender who does not wish to reoffend. This segment of the program should be perceived as a separate and critical component of the total treatment program. Programs that incorporate gradual, monitored release into the treatment agenda provide the opportunity for the "shaky" offender to be pulled back into the program when he begins to exhibit old preoffense patterns.

GOAL SIX

Each sex offender needs access to a post-treatment group for assistance in maintaining a safe lifestyle. Most programs provide some kind of therapeutic support for the client after he has graduated from the program. At least, there is usually a hotline, while others may permit the graduate to attend his former group or make provisions for him to meet with the program therapist on an individual basis.

A troublesome situation is where the young person has completed a residential program and lives far from the treatment facility where no community-based treatment service is available. It is essential to maintain a network of adolescent specialized treatment services statewide so that the program graduate can continue to monitor and upgrade his new acquired behaviors.

TREATMENT SUCCESS

This very brief outline of goals and types of treatment for adolescent sex offenders raises a primary question: Does it work? Until longitudinal research is undertaken and standardized measures of treatment outcome are established, it will be difficult to assess the treatment variables that enable adolescent sex offenders to control their sexually aggressive behaviors.

Nevertheless, out of their cumulative experience, adolescent sex-offender treatment specialists generally agree that 1) early intervention in these compulsive behaviors is most important and useful; and that 2) offenders who have been exposed to programs that provide the skills and tools for them to recognize and manage their sexually aggressive behaviors have a much greater chance of controlling impulses and leading nonassaultive lives than those who have not had such treatment.

Further, preliminary results reported by programs treating youthful sex offenders indicate a low number of known repeat offenses. These include:

1. Contributors to the Uniform Data Collection System of the National Adolescent Perpetrator Network provided follow-up data on 69 cases of sexual offenses by adolescents. In the 12-30 months after their clients had left the specialized sex-offender treatment programs, 90.8% were not known to have recommitted a sexual offense; 9.2% had been either re-arrested or questioned in regard to a sexual offense since ending treatment. This was less than clinical impressions had predicted (Ryan & Miyoshi, 1990).

2. The Program for Healthy Adolescent Sexual Expression (PHASE) in Maplewood, Minnesota, a nonresidential program, reports that as of 1990, of 200 follow-ups of adolescents who completed the program, 94% were not known to have recommitted a sexual offense. Of the 6% who were known to have recommitted a sexual offense, 2.5% had acted out sexually while in assessment or treatment; the remaining 3.5% acted out after completing the treatment program (O'Brien, 1990).

3. The Hennepin County Home School, in Minnetonka, Minnesota, a residential program for sex offenders involved in serious offenses, reports that follow-ups of 149 of the 285 sex offenders who participated in the specialized program since April 1982 indicate that 11% were known to have recommitted a sexual offense (Bremer, 1990).

On the whole, these are encouraging statistics.

Section Five
STATE PLANNING

WHILE THE TREATMENT OPTIONS THAT now exist around the country have evolved in quite different ways, the need for and usefulness of these services have been so clearly established that private and public authorities in many states and counties are now beginning to respond. In an effort to take a comprehensive look at the whole problem of juvenile/adolescent sex offenses and public responses to them, some states are establishing task forces to 1) determine the number of known youthful sex offenders in both official and nonofficial data, 2) determine the present response of the system, at all levels, to these assaults, and 3) plan for comprehensive remedial intervention.

State planning for comprehensive remedial intervention should include:

1. The development of a capacity for training specialists in the public and private sectors to assess, evaluate, and treat adolescent sex offenders;

2. The development of a specialized capability to assess all adolescent sex offenders prior to adjudication so that recommendations for appropriate placement and treatment can be offered the court before sentencing occurs;

3. The provision of fiscal and staff support for networking among treatment providers, victim-service specialists, and related criminal justice personnel;

4. In all major cities and counties, the availability of

public and private community-based outpatient services to all adolescent sex offenders who are evaluated as appropriate for community placement;

5. The special training of probation and parole officers in the issues involved with adolescent sex-offender patterns and treatment so that compliance with the specialized conditions of sentencing can be monitored;

6. The establishment of residential, therapeutic communities for the serious adolescent sex offender, either in the private or public sector, with special provisions for those few who require more secure treatment settings;

7. The provision of very gradual, monitored release from residential treatment programs;

8. The inclusion of a research component that standardizes the collection of data, establishes offense typologies, and measures treatment outcomes;

9. Education about the issues involved in these behaviors, since the public and many officials are not well informed about youthful sex offenders;

10. Development of a comprehensive prevention strategy, integrating treatment as one component.

There is no longer any valid excuse for ignoring and neglecting a public safety issue as obvious and important as the treatment of adolescent sex offenders. To acknowledge the importance of this problem requires our constructive response. By recognizing these behaviors, validating their seriousness, demanding accountability from the young offender, and providing the necessary specialized treatment, we have taken the first steps toward controlling and reducing sexual assault.

REFERENCES

Abel, G.G. (1984, February). *The outcome of assessment treatment at the Sexual Clinic and its relevance to the need for treatment programs for adolescent sex offenders in New York state.* Paper presented at a Safer Society Program press briefing, Albany, NY.

Abel, G.G. (1983, December). *Sexual offenders: Results of assessment and recommendations for treatment.* Paper presented at a meeting of the World Congress of Behavior Therapy.

American Psychiatric Association. (1980). *Diagnostic & statistical manual of mental disorders* (3rd ed.). Washington, DC: American Psychiatric Association.

Becker, J.V., & Abel, G.G. (1984). Methodological and ethical issues in evaluation and treating adolescent sexual offenders. *National Institute of Mental Health Monograph* (June).

Bremer, J. (1990) Personal communication to F.H. Knopp, October.

Groth, A.N., Longo, R.E., & McFadin, J.B. (1982). Undetected recidivism among rapists & child molesters. *Crime & Delinquency, 28*(3).

Groth, A.N., & Loredo, C.M. (1981). Juvenile sex offenders: Guidelines for assessment. *International Journal of Offender Therapy & Comparative Criminology, 25*(1).

Haversack, G. (1984) Personal communication to F.H. Knopp, April.

Knopp, F.H. (1984). *Retraining adult sex offenders: Methods & models.* Orwell, VT: Safer Society Press.

Knopp, F.H. (1982). *Remedial intervention in adolescent sex offenses: Nine program descriptions.* Orwell, VT: Safer Society Press.

Knopp, F.H., & Stevenson, W.F. (1989). *Nationwide survey of juvenile & adult sex-offender treatment programs, 1988.* Orwell, VT: Safer Society Press.

Knopp, F.H., & Stevenson, W.F. (1990). *Nationwide survey of juvenile & adult sex-offender treatment programs & models, 1990.* Orwell, VT: Safer Society Press.

Longo, R.E., & Groth, A.N. *(1982). Juvenile sex offenses in the histories of adult rapists and child* molesters. Unpublished manuscript.

National Adolescent Perpetrator Network. (1988). Preliminary report from the National Task Force on juvenile sexual offending 1988. *Juvenile & Family Court Journal, 39*(2).

O'Brien, M. (1990). Personal communication to F.H. Knopp, October.

Ryan, G., & Miyoshi, T. (1990). Summary of a pilot follow-up study of adolescent sexual perpetrators after treatment. *Interchange,* January.

Smith, W.R. *(1985, May). Juvenile sex offenders and the prediction of risk.* Paper presented at the meeting of The Kempe Center and the National Center for the Prevention and Control of Rape/ National Institute for Mental Health, Keystone, Colorado.

Other SAFER SOCIETY Publications

37 to One: Living as an Integrated Multiple by Phoenix J. Hocking (1996). $12.00.

The Brother/Sister Hurt: Recognizing the Effects of Sibling Abuse by Vernon Wiehe, PhD (1996). $10.00.

Adult Sex Offender Assessment Packet by Mark Carich & Donya Adkerson (1995). $8.00.

Empathy and Compassionate Action: Issues & Exercises: A Workbook for Clients in Treatment by Robert Freeman-Longo, Laren Bays, & Euan Bear (1995). $12.00.

The Difficult Connection: The Therapeutic Relationship in Sex Offender Treatment by Geral T. Blanchard (1995). $10.00.

Men & Anger: A Guide to Understanding and Managing Your Anger for a Much Better Life by Murray Cullen & Robert Freeman-Longo (1996). $15.00.

Shining Through: Pulling It Together After Sexual Abuse by Mindy Loiselle & Leslie Bailey Wright (1995). $12.00. (A workbook especially for girls ages 10 through 16.)

From Trauma to Understanding: A Guide for Parents of Children with Sexual Behavior Problems by William D. Pithers, Alison S. Gray, Carolyn Cunningham, & Sandy Lane (1993). $5.00.

Adolescent Sexual Offender Assessment Packet by Alison Stickrod Gray & Randy Wallace (1992). $8.00.

The Relapse Prevention Workbook for Youth in Treatment by Charlene Steen (1993). $15.00.

Pathways: A Guided Workbook for Youth Beginning Treatment by Timothy J. Kahn (1990; revised 1992; 3rd printing). $15.00.

Pathways Guide for Parents of Youth Beginning Treatment by Timothy J. Kahn (1990). $9.50.

Man-to-Man, When Your Partner Says NO: Pressured Sex & Date Rape by Scott Allen Johnson (1992). $6.50.

When Your Wife Says No: Forced Sex in Marriage by Fay Honey Knopp (1994). $7.00.

Female Adolescent Sexual Abusers: An Exploratory Study of Mother-Daughter Dynamics with Implications for Treatment by Marcia T. Turner & Tracey N. Turner (1994). $18.00.

Who Am I & Why Am I in Treatment? A Guided Workbook for Clients in Evaluation and Beginning Treatment by Robert Freeman-Longo & Laren Bays (1988; 7th printing). $12.00.

Why Did I Do It Again? Understanding My Cycle of Problem Behaviors by Laren Bays & Robert Freeman-Longo (1989; 5th printing). $12.00.

How Can I Stop? Breaking My Deviant Cycle by Laren Bays, Robert Freeman-Longo, & Diane Hildebran (1990; 4th printing). $12.00.

Adults Molested As Children: A Survivor's Manual for Women & Men by Euan Bear with Peter Dimock (1988; 4th printing). $12.95.

Family Fallout: A Handbook for Families of Adult Sexual Abuse Survivors by Dorothy Beaulieu Landry, MEd. (1991). $12.95.

Embodying Healing: Integrated Bodywork and Psychotherapy in Recovery from Childhood Sexual Abuse by Robert J. Timms, PhD, and Patrick Connors, CMT. (1992). $15.00.

The Safer Society publishes additional books, audiocassettes, and training videos related to the treatment of sexual abuse. A catalog of our complete listings is available.

THE SAFER SOCIETY PRESS
PO BOX 340 • BRANDON, VERMONT 05733-0340
TELEPHONE (802) 247-3132

ORDER FORM

Date_____

SHIPPING ADDRESS: ☐ *Please send a catalog*

Name and/or Agency_____

Address *(location only — no PO box)* _____

_____

City_____ State_____ Zip_____

MAILING ADDRESS *(if different from shipping address)*:

Address_____

City_____ State_____ Zip_____

Daytime Phone (_____) _____

QTY	TITLE	UNIT PRICE	TOTAL COST

	SUB TOTAL	
U.S. funds only.	**VT RESIDENTS ADD SALES TAX**	
Make checks payable to: SAFER SOCIETY PRESS	**SHIPPING** *(SEE BELOW)*	
	TOTAL	

U.S. funds only.

Make checks payable to:
SAFER SOCIETY PRESS

All prices subject to change without notice.

NO RETURNS.

Mail to:
SAFER SOCIETY PRESS
PO Box 340
Brandon, Vermont 05733-0340
(802) 247-3132

Shipping:
Add 8% to all orders for shipping & handling.

Rush Orders: Add $10.00.

Bulk Order discounts available.

Phone orders accepted with VISA/MasterCard.